MY CAPE IS AT THE CLEANERS

Choosing Happy over Perfect

By Wendy Elover

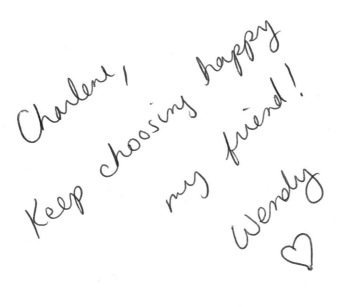

Charlene,
Keep choosing happy
my friend!

Wendy
♡

Special Note about Your Purchase

Thank you for purchasing a copy of *My Cape Is at the Cleaners*.

A portion of the proceeds from my book sales will support **Believe Big,** (**www.believebig.org**), an incredible organization dedicated to helping patients and their families navigate through the cancer journey.

I invite you to visit **www.wendyelover.com** and join **My Insider's List** for additional bonuses and updates.

Interested in a bulk purchase of books for your company, organization or community group?

Interested in having me come and speak at your convention, business meeting, organization or community group?

Contact me at: **wendy@wendyelover.com**

My Cape Is at the Cleaners

DEDICATION

This book is dedicated to my family.

To my three amazing daughters, **Nicole, Julie, and Shannon,** who teach me about life on a daily basis and inspire me to become the very best version of myself that I can. You make me laugh, and you make my heart smile. I can't wait to see what the future holds for each of you. You are all strong, intelligent, uniquely beautiful souls, and I feel blessed to be your mom.

To my husband, **Marc,** who has been by my side through the good, the bad, and everything in-between for almost 30 years. You put up with my never-ending stream of wild and crazy plans, and you allow me the freedom to keep reaching for my dreams, even when you don't always understand the plan or know what's coming next. I am thankful for your kind and generous heart, your silly (and endless) puns, and your "creative" song lyrics. Most importantly, I am grateful for your unconditional love. I love you forever plus 60 years.

ACKNOWLEDGEMENTS

There's an African proverb that says, "It takes a village to raise a child." I am so lucky to be surrounded by an incredible group of women helping my family through the craziness of daily life.

Thank you for always being a light in the darkness and for helping me through the roughest times, and for also always being there with me to celebrate the little victories along the way. I treasure your friendship. My life is richer because you're in it.

Thank you to **Dr. Ashley Block, Shari Cohen, Anna Coleman, Sylvia Kellman, Lana Koman, Amy Lebowitz, Elaine Lee, Jennifer Millman, Laila O'Brien, Rabbi Dana Saroken, Karen Stevenson and the Parents of the Hero's TLC 2021 Green Team**.

To my accountability partners **Beth Bracaglia, April Force Pardoe, Laila O'Brien and Elena Emmart**: thank you for always believing in me, holding me to my word, coaxing me along when I wanted to give in, and continually keeping me moving forward. You are each a blessing in my life.

Thank you to my **amazing circle of business networking friends and my Academy Mortgage teammates**. You inspire and challenge me, you lift me up, and you encourage me daily. I am in awe of you and so thankful to have each of you in my world.

To my mom, **Mindy Laufer**, and my dad, **Nat Kellman**: thank you for teaching me how to stand on my own while at the same time, always providing me with a safe place to land. You made me believe I could be anything I wanted to be, and you taught me the importance of hard work, loyalty, and love. Even though you've left this earth, I carry you both in my heart always and miss and love you every day.

TABLE OF CONTENTS

A MESSAGE FROM ME TO YOU

I am a work in progress, filled with flaws and imperfections. There, I said it. I am not perfect. This may seem like a silly (and obvious) proclamation to many of you, but for me, after spending much of my life trying to live up to the be-it-all, do-it-all mentality, this is a big step forward.

We all carry labels, whether we impose them on ourselves or we take them from others. I am a mother, a wife, a daughter, a caregiver, and a fixer of all things amongst many others.

Until a few years ago, the best description of me would be an overworked, overstressed, do-it-all perfectionist with a lack of true focus. I desperately clung to my to-do list along with my should-do list and must-do list.

These labels gave me definition in my daily life and provided me with guidance, structure, and even comfort. They defined who I was and what I was supposed to do daily. However, I've come to realize these labels are also potentially dangerous. They pigeonhole us and categorize us, stopping us from spreading our wings and dreaming beyond our current circumstances.

When I decided to write this book, I knew in order to write what I really wanted to share with you, I needed to, once and for all, give up my need to keep up my perfect persona (even though it probably only existed in my mind), and instead, be totally real and share with you the not-so-flattering stories from my own life. I hope through sharing the good AND the bad, you will see that we all have incredible power to create our lives on purpose if we're willing to take control of our minds and take responsibility for our actions.

In many different shapes and forms, we are each striving to become the person we are meant to be amidst all the everyday chaos in our lives. The challenge is that we are so busy rushing around to get things done and taking care of others that, for many of us, it's been years since we've thought about the person we'd like to grow into or the life we'd like to create for ourselves.

This is my story: my challenges, lessons learned, and small daily victories. At a minimum, I hope this book will let you take a few moments to breathe and give you a few smiles and laughs along the way. Within these pages, you may even catch a small glimpse of your own life or grab a new idea that helps you find the strength and determination to leave some of your "have to's" and "must do's" behind.

If you haven't already, I hope you will finally give yourself permission to reclaim your time and dream again, creating a life you enjoy every day filled with happiness, peace, and all the amazing things your heart and mind can imagine.

Life is short. Let's enjoy the journey together!

With gratitude,

Wendy

"The greatest source of happiness is the ability to be grateful at all times."

Zig Ziglar

GETTING TO KNOW EACH OTHER

"I myself am made entirely of flaws,
stitched together with good intentions."
Augusten Burroughs

Since I'm about to give you a pretty intimate "behind the curtain" look at my life, I figure it's important for you to know I'm a real person with a real life filled with ups, downs, and a whole lot of crazy! So here's a quick overview of me...

I grew up in the Baltimore, Maryland area and met my life-long best friend, Ashley, when I was 3 years old. We've been friends ever since, which is especially good for me because (1) she knows way too much about me to have her wandering out in the world unsupervised, and (2) she holds half my brain and stores most of my childhood memories.

My mom and dad got divorced when I was young. Although it was a hard time, I'm thankful they were strong enough to make the tough decision to move on and go after the lives they imagined. They both found love again and each remarried, giving me a ton of awesome brothers and sisters

and showing me what a happy marriage looks like from the inside-out.

Watching their journey taught me many life lessons: the importance of staying true to yourself; learning to stand on your own (and when NOT to); the power of stepping outside your comfort zone even when you're scared beyond measure; and finally, that it's possible to work together for a common goal (in their case, raising me) even when it's not a "perfect" situation.

My dad had an appliance repair business when I was little, so I learned to fix washers, dryers, and dishwashers at an early age. I developed a love of working with tools and taking things apart which has served me well over the years. Most of the time when I disassemble things, I can actually manage to put them back together again, often with a few "extra" parts left over.

When I was 16, to earn gas money, my first real job was doing singing telegrams in a belly-dancing gorilla suit. Many adventures were had and life lessons learned peering out at the world through a fuzzy gorilla head.

I am a MAJOR klutz! I fall UP the stairs in my house regularly, and I actually cracked the front of my skull (according to the MRI) walking into a pole at a professional baseball game.

I like chocolate: chocolate candy, chocolate cake, chocolate mousse. If it's chocolate, I like it. If you give it to me, I will like YOU by association.

I'm not a big fan of cooking, but I'm a huge fan of eating, so I cook on an "as needed" basis. My crockpot is my trusted companion along with my collection of take-out menus.

I have three amazing daughters, including a set of fraternal twins. They were the first girls in my husband's family in over 90 years, and they are each here, in part, thanks to the amazing medical technology advances of in vitro fertilization (IVF). They are funny, smart, and truly unique individuals, and they know how to push every one of my buttons like no one else can. They are my heart and my reason for all that I do, and I'm so thankful for each of them.

I firmly believe that unconditional love is one of the greatest gifts you can share with another human being. Without it, I don't know how my dear hubby would have put up with all my antics over the past 30 years. I guess that's also how he manages to survive in our household filled with four strong-willed females.

I cry at the drop of a hat—happy, sad, angry—it all requires Kleenex for me. When a sappy holiday coffee commercial comes on, I'll be wiping away the tears.

I'd much rather be speaking to you than writing this. I'm a "live-and-in-person" kind of gal, but I'm humbled and honored that you're taking the time to read and share this journey with me.

Although my life is far from rainbows and butterflies, even on my worst days I am blessed beyond belief, and I try to appreciate and share that gratitude daily.

1

WHAT DO YOU WANT TO BE WHEN YOU GROW UP?

"The meaning of life is to find your gift.
The purpose of life is to give it away."

Picasso

When you were little, somewhere, someone probably asked you, "What do you want to be when you grow up?" You probably responded with an answer like a doctor, a teacher, an astronaut, or a famous movie star. What you probably did NOT say was, "I want to be a stressed out, overworked, underpaid and exhausted grownup whose life is overflowing with obligations and responsibilities and seriously lacking in *me* time and fun."

So how did it happen? How did we go from innocent, happy, laughing children to adults spending too much time working, worrying, and spinning our wheels instead of actually living the life we once imagined?

In my own life, as the years went by, I started to accept this fate as the natural progression of more have-to's and less choices. If that's your answer right now, I want you to know I understand. Life can be rough and challenging at times, and can sometimes feel like one long endless day. Believe me, I've been there. Some days, I'm STILL there, but not nearly as often as I once was. I've had more than a few times when I wondered how I was going to make it through the next day, week, or even hour, and I questioned down to my core why life had done this to me.

The good news is, while it may be hard to believe right now, life doesn't have to be that way, and things can start changing right now. No matter what your current circumstances are or where you are currently in your life, there is a way out of the funk. However, as I've discovered first-hand, no matter how many books you buy or self-help seminars you attend, life doesn't change until you personally decide (and commit) to changing it. And when I say decide, I'm not talking about thinking for a few minutes, "Gee, wouldn't it be nice if things were different," or even deciding that you'll TRY to change.

Nope. I "tried" for many years, and I can tell you nothing substantial or life-altering happened. I stayed stuck until I finally took a realistic (rather scary and somewhat painful) look at my own life and decided that staying stuck where I was seemed actually scarier than stepping out of my comfort zone to become someone capable of living the life I imagined.

"Do or do not. There is no try." -Yoda

Now right about now, I'm guessing you're probably either thinking, "Yeah! I'm in! Let's get started!" OR you're muttering to yourself, "Oh no! Is this going to be another one of those 'think yourself happy' books?" Either way, I hope you'll keep reading.

Sometimes in those moments when we feel the most vulnerable, the most exposed, and even the most defeated, we are only moments away from our most incredible, life-changing breakthroughs and accomplishments if we just...keep…going!

"When you are tempted to give up, your breakthrough is probably just around the corner." - Joyce Meyer

2

CREATING LIFE
BACKWARDS ON PURPOSE

*"You are never too old to set another goal
or to dream a new dream."*
C. S. Lewis

Have you ever had a sleepless night where you watched the infomercials on late night TV?

"Get rock hard abs in 21 days!"

"Lose 10 pounds in 10 days!"

"Drop a dress size in a week!"

Whether or not you actually believe the specific claims, I realized this slick marketing message style had infiltrated my daily life.

My desire for the quick fix (instant gratification) had created a dangerous thought pattern in my brain that I was completely oblivious to at the time.

If you've ever read any type of personal development book, you've probably encountered at least one chapter about goals. There's usually a suggestion to set long-term goals in each of a few areas of your life: finances, relationships, health, etc.

While I think this is quite a valid idea in theory, whenever I personally tried to set goals for myself, some unnamed and unexplained force would stop me in my tracks.

My intentions, at least on the outside, were there. I took all the appropriate steps to prepare to make big changes...and then NOTHING! I was baffled. I consider myself a relatively intelligent human capable of some sort of competent thought, so why couldn't I complete such a seemingly simple task? I was stuck, but I had no idea why or how to fix my situation.

I tried reading (ok, skimming through) lots of self-help books, and while the information was interesting and somewhat compelling, I was still no closer to a breakthrough.

I stared at the clean white-lined page, excited to start outlining my goals and to create my new destiny. But hours later, I was still looking at the same blank paper. Funny how sometimes the answers are right in front of you, but you still can't see them.

The Appointment
That Changed Everything

After months of dragging my heels, I had finally scheduled an appointment to discuss my money matters. It was not an appointment I was looking forward to, and I had actually rescheduled (and almost cancelled) several times. But something about this new networking friend of mine, Laila O'Brien, made me keep this appointment on that day.

She wasn't like other financial gurus I had met. She said she and her husband were focused on educating the middle class (i.e., the ones who didn't have $500,000 to invest, but had plenty of credit card debt and bills to go around!). She said she believed we could all be financially successful if we just took time to learn the rules of "the money game," and then work the plan.

"Most people don't plan to fail; they fail to plan."

– John L. Beckley

While it sounded like a noble mission, and I certainly fit her target demographic at the time, I was still quite skeptical. Honestly, I was beyond mortified at the thought of sharing my years of financial screw-ups (this went SO against my need to maintain my outside perfect persona). However, I had made the appointment, and it was too late to cancel now. That would be rude. So, with a stomach full of knots, I took a breath, determined to politely go in AND get out as quickly and painlessly as I could with as much of my dignity intact as possible.

Little did I know that this short meeting would impact my future life in ways I couldn't even begin to imagine.

My outward mission was simple and well-defined: to discuss my financial plans—or more accurately, my LACK of financial plans—and how to take steps to better my current situation and get my family on the path to financial freedom. What I hadn't yet realized is how my inward voice was battling to avoid any conversation that didn't put me in the best light. Yes, this was going to be an interesting encounter.

I walked into the office, and there was Laila, smiling as always, full of enthusiasm and warmth, trying so hard to put me at ease—an impossible task at this point.

After a bit of standard chit-chat, Laila gave me a big, sincere, comforting smile from across her desk, and casually spoke, "Imagine if money and time were no issue. Put on your dream hat and tell me about what your life would look like."

Sounds simple enough, right? And I'm guessing for many of you, this would be an easy, even fun task, but in that moment, I was completely paralyzed. I had NOTHING to say (and I ALWAYS have something to say!). It suddenly hit me right between the eyes. This feeling of being stuck—I suddenly got my first hint at its root. Somewhere along the way to becoming an adult, without even noticing it, I had given up on my dreams, little by little, and I had let them fade away. As my dreams disappeared, so did my ability to set and achieve any solid, life-changing goals.

If you can't even imagine that life can get better, how can you possibly make any plans to actually change it?

While this new revelation happened quite suddenly and unexpectedly, I realized that all the previous actions that had led me to this current situation had not been nearly so obvious. Instead, it had been more of a slow, subtle, sneaky process that had happened over many years as my busy everyday schedule and my daily struggle to make it all look easy and under control (at least on the outside) had taken over every available bit of space in my brain, leaving no room to dream, plan, or grow.

One business idea didn't quite work, so instead of adjusting my plans, I just gave up that idea. One life goal I wanted to achieve suddenly didn't seem possible with the added responsibilities of marriage and a family, so again, instead of looking at it from a different angle, I just let it go.

"When obstacles arise, you change your direction to reach your goals; you do not change your decision to get there." - Zig Ziglar

While none of these individual events appeared to be life-altering when they were going on, I now realize that without the ability to dream, you lose the ability to set goals. And without setting goals, it's nearly impossible to achieve anything substantial, and it most certainly isn't possible to create a life by design.

"If you don't know where you're going, you're bound to end up someplace else." - Yogi Berra

In that one instant, sitting there with Laila's simple question swirling around my brain, it became crystal clear to me that if I wanted to have the amazing life I had once imagined, I was going to have to start at ground zero and rediscover how to dream again. But where to begin?

Trying to choose what to focus on and imagine my "dream life" at this point in time was absolutely 100% an impossible task. I had lost too much confidence and had experienced too many disappointments to be able to just suddenly start describing the ultimate dream life that I had once imagined for myself and for my family, but had given up on years ago.

Maybe you've had a similar experience at some point. That vague, uncomfortable feeling that something is missing, but you can't quite figure it out. You're moving through everyday life, perhaps even outwardly thriving, but inside, you feel lost and out of control, and you don't even know quite why.

In that brief moment, I realized I had a choice to make. I could either give up dreaming entirely and accept the life I was currently in forever, or I could take the uncomfortable and scary next step, begin editing what my mind's eye could imagine, and then somehow figure out how to go from that picture to my new reality.

Both options seemed unbelievably daunting in different ways. I was scared down to my core. I felt overwhelmed, unprepared and ill-equipped to face the road ahead. BUT the idea of staying stuck forever where I was right now seemed even more frightening and horrifying than taking this next leap into the unknown...so I decided to jump! It was the first of many leaps to come.

Baby Steps....Learning to Live for Me Again

I realized that over the years, I had created quite a massive, yet invisible, rule book (mostly existing in my head) filled with endless lists of responsibilities and should-do's. My days were full, and I wore my busy-ness like a badge of honor, even though all this mindless activity was getting me nowhere and leaving me feeling like a constant failure.

I had blindly fallen into a self-destructive pattern of failing to nurture and pay attention to my own needs and desires. Instead, I focused every ounce of my available time and energy trying to be "good" and doing what was expected of me. I took on the full-time role of caregiver and fixer of all problems, even when no one was actually requesting my help.

As my mind slowly started to open up, I began to see a glimpse of the possibility that there could be more—a lot more—for me than the life I was currently living. Little by little, I began to realize that the person I used to be was not necessarily the person I was going to become.

I slowly, and with a great deal of fear and apprehension, started to give myself permission to step out of the strict mold I had created for myself. I was caught off guard when I found that along with this self-permission came an amazing and much needed freedom I hadn't experienced in years.

This newly found freedom allowed me to start (slowly) letting go of some of my past mistakes and disappointments, and without all that baggage, I started to imagine what the new me could achieve.

"What you get by achieving your goals is not nearly as important as who you become by achieving your goals." - Zig Ziglar

I started small. I started dreaming very small at first. I picked financial goals that were almost laughable, but at the time seemed challenging. I imagined small changes in my family's everyday life too. But I quickly began to realize that small dreams would lead to a small life. If I ever wanted to live the big life I hoped and dreamed of in my mind, I was going to have to learn to dream bigger—much bigger. But how?

The Dreaded 4 Letter "F-Word"

Nothing was actually wrong with my everyday life. In fact, to many around me, my life was pretty darn near perfect.

How are the kids? FINE.
How's your husband? FINE.
How's work? FINE.
How's life in general? FINE.

Yup. The life I was living every day was…FINE.

No big issues. No huge catastrophes. I had settled into my "fine" life, floating along each day complacent, with no urgency or push to change.

I had started to settle. I had work that was "adequate" along with a level of success that was "good enough." My home life and relationships with my family and friends were "fine."

But was this really the big life I had dreamed of long ago? It was time to shake things up.

Learning to Dream BIG Again

I had heard the advice to "dream big" so many times that it never dawned on me that dreaming, and especially dreaming big, was a skill and not something we have from birth. Actually, after thinking about it further, I realized it is probably something we ARE born with but slowly lose along the way.

When you speak with young children about what they imagine their life to be in the future, most of them will tell you quite a tale about where they will live, who they will marry, what job they will have, and how successful they will be in their life.

As I accumulated life experiences including my share of setbacks, resistance and even failures, I started losing belief in my young mind's plans. Without the proper mindset and skills in place to reevaluate and adjust my plans, I had, without even consciously noticing, given up, little by little, on my dreams.

I was living a life that I'd somehow created without any actual intention or direction. Something had to change, and it had to begin within me. I had to relearn how to dream and then set goals to make those dreams come true. It sounded simple at first, but I quickly realized that there is a big difference between having a dream, setting a goal, and actually achieving things in your life.

> **"A dream written down with a DATE, becomes a goal. A goal broken down into STEPS, becomes a plan. A plan backed by ACTION makes your dream come true!" - Greg S. Reid**

Upgrading My Circle

Since I had clearly determined that I was definitely no expert in the dreaming and goal-setting arena, I realized I was going to need some guidance as I ventured into this untapped territory. I knew that finding the right people at this stage could make or break my success.

I also realized I was going to have to, once again, put my ego aside, let go of my perfect persona mindset, and allow myself to be vulnerable and ask for help. As a caregiver and fixer-of-all-problems (at least that's what I believed), this was a painful yet necessary step towards regaining my footing and recapturing my ability to dream.

"We are a combination of the 5 people we spend the most time with." - Jim Rohn

I was lucky enough to be surrounded by some amazing, strong, inspiring role models, and I encourage you right now to take an honest look at the folks you spend the majority of your "free" time with daily. If you truly want to change your life, you may also need to upgrade that circle. While I'm certainly not suggesting that you drop your long-time best friends, I definitely do strongly urge you to consider how and where each of those people fit into the life you are designing on purpose.

With so much of my life feeling out of my control, I clung onto the idea that at least my attitude was 100% within my control. Since I was starting to realize that attitudes were contagious, I knew I was going to need to focus on constantly surrounding myself with people who would lift me up, inspire me, and push me to be the best possible version of myself every minute of every day. Plus, at this point, I desperately needed people who believed in me and believed in the new and improved life I was working to create, even if I wasn't yet fully convinced myself.

I became even more determined to find others who were a step ahead of me, and who would be willing and able to help me learn and grow to become the person I needed to become to create the life and the impact I was now determined to achieve.

At first, I saw this amazing group of people as far superior to me, high up on a pedestal, attaining things completely out of my reach. I had a hard time connecting the dots as to how my current life situation related and was

20

intertwined in any meaningful way with theirs. But as I began to learn to dream again, the gap between these people and myself started to decrease and eventually fade away.

As I envisioned big things for myself again, and my mind's eye started to believe in the possibilities, my need to start moving these ideas forward and design the life I was imagining became more and more urgent to me. It no longer was an option; it was a "have to," and the sooner it happened, the better!

Finding My "Whys"

I had always thought of goals as far off lofty achievements, almost impossible to attain. I pictured goals as the ultimate prize at the top of a very tall, very steep mountain. And for those who know me well, I'm no mountain climber!

I'd blindly leave my safe stance on solid ground with a vague goal way at the top. From my point of view, I couldn't see more than a few hundred feet ahead, so it was easy to quickly lose sight of the mountain top (aka goal).

I had no strong "whys" in place to make my success imperative. I had no action steps to keep me moving forward when things went wrong along the way. Plus, I had years and years of memories of times I had come up short, and these memories popped up every time I encountered even the smallest challenge.

It's not surprising that each time I started towards a goal, it wouldn't take long for fear, doubt, and feelings of inevitable defeat to creep in and stop me in my tracks. The climb was too hard, too long, and filled with too many roadblocks I wasn't prepared to face and conquer.

Ok, so I knew I needed a purpose, a determined focused reason to push myself. I needed better, stronger, more important whys.

I decided to create a vision board. I gathered pictures of my family, my friends, and I searched online for quotes and pictures that would inspire me. Armed with my glue stick and scissors, I set out to start re-creating my dreams. I hung the board over my desk where I would see it daily to hopefully give me the push I needed to move forward.

As I slowly imagined possible changes, I also became frustrated and angry at myself for taking so long to realize this unproductive and self-sabotaging pattern. I started dwelling on how different my life could have been if I had noticed and addressed this issue sooner.

It would have been so easy at this point to fall back into my old, comfortable (yet unproductive) patterns of blame, sadness, and defeat, but something inside of me was slowly but surely beginning to change.

"Dwelling on past bad decisions you've made only allows those decisions to keep defining you. Forgive yourself and move on." - Mandy Hale

I reminded myself that I can't change the past, but that maybe, just maybe, I could start to change my future. I began to ask myself... Is there another way? What's missing in this plan? Where do I go from here or is this all there is for me?

Maybe you've experienced something similar in your life. Situations change, daily routines sneak in when you're not looking, and suddenly all the magical, fun, exciting dreams you imagined for yourself slowly drift away, leaving you feeling stuck, sad, and defeated before you even begin.

I quickly realized that for me, even if it hadn't been a conscious effort with a name and a plan, my whole life had been a series of "regrouping" sessions—I just didn't yet have the skills and the vision to use these moments to my advantage to move me forward instead of bringing me to a screeching halt. Most of my earlier attempts at accomplishing truly big goals had sent me quickly running full speed down the hill to safety, never looking back.

I knew if I had any chance at all of moving forward, I first needed to take the time to consciously quiet my mind enough to build strong, powerful, meaningful, solid whys.

These whys would help me keep moving forward even when potential roadblocks and challenges appeared. Over time, I hoped these whys would also help me regain my strength and confidence to reach for the dreams I had abandoned along the way.

I knew my old method of trying to set goals was not working, so I needed a new and better way to begin.

I knew in the past, my big goals felt overwhelming and unattainable, so this time, I tried breaking my big ideas down into smaller, more manageable chunks, and giving myself permission to take breaks and regroup as needed.

"When eating an elephant, take one bite at a time." - Creighton Abrams

Next, I decided that, for me, a long-term, huge goal was too far away and invisible to keep me motivated daily, so I would need to find lots of reasons to celebrate the little, smaller mini-triumphs along the way. I needed to regain control and actively and intentionally take action.

23

While all of this sounded great and wonderful in theory, this whole process led me straight back to the basics to question how, why and even IF I even should be setting "traditional" goals at all.

I knew learning to dream again was a vital skill I needed to relearn, but a dream is just that—a dream, an invisible thought of something you would like or desire to have. But as I had previously experienced way too often in my life, unless your name is Aladdin and you happen to find a magic lamp, we don't just dream of something and suddenly have it show up in our lives. I realized that to turn those dreams into results, I was going to have to do the hard work. I needed a plan of action!

Come Take a Walk with Me

Soon after, a networking friend mentioned she was reading a new book by Hal Elrod, *The Miracle Morning*. She told me this book had introduced her to a whole new way to start and focus her day. She used words like *life-altering* and *game-changing*. As usual, I had a healthy skepticism, but I was interested in seeing what this book was all about.

Being a hopeless multitasker at heart, instead of sitting down to read his book, I popped in my headphones and began listening to a few of his podcasts during my morning walks.

As I continued listening to Hal Elrod's podcasts, he shared his incredible story of surviving a horrific car accident that left him dead for 6 minutes. Ironically, according to Hal, that was NOT his rock bottom. I began reading about his "miracle morning" routine and ideas, and as I did, I felt my foggy mind start to clear. I swear I could almost feel the individual neurons re-connecting in my brain as I tried to soak in and recall every last word and concept I was listening to each morning.

Along with listening to Hal's many stories and guest interviews, I started to find other authors and podcasts that inspired me, and I incorporated reading and listening to these early each morning as part of the kick-off to my day.

While I was still putting in long hours and waking up even earlier than I had previously (partly at Hal's suggestion and partly because I was desperate to find additional moments in my day), I began to feel a new level of positivity and energy throughout my day. I would come back after my walk and furiously scribble all my thoughts about what I had listened to that morning. As my mind cleared, an amazing thing happened. For the first time in more years than I care to admit, I began to see my dreams clearly again.

Turning Dreams into Action

I started creating goals for myself based on those dreams. I got a cheap binder and some notebook paper and started scribbling down practically every dream that popped into my head and the goals associated with it.

I knew it was important to set timelines and assign dates to my goals, but once again, I found myself stuck until I gave myself permission to think outside the box and find a solution that would work for me.

Perhaps the reason I was having so much trouble assigning dates to all my goals was that I had created two very different types of goals: time-sensitive goals AND "until" goals.

The time-sensitive goals were more straightforward. Beside each one, I wrote down a date: 30 days, 60 days, 90 days, 6 months, a year, etc.

For the few remaining goals, my "until" goals, I accepted that I would need to let go of the scheduled, organized, "perfect" side of myself, and accept that these goals were so big, and required so much creative time and energy, that I would need to devote myself to them 110% UNTIL I accomplished each and every one of them regardless of the time frame involved.

I knew this set of goals would present me with the greatest challenges and potential roadblocks and barriers, and that there would be times throughout this whole process where I would feel defeated or unable to keep fighting, but these goals were non-negotiable.

These were my true game-changing life goals, and they were absolutely, positively required to be achieved, just not in a specific time frame.

The trick was that although these goals had no defined timing, it was imperative that my everyday plans included actions and steps that would continue to move these big goals forward.

To really get a sense of what goals I needed to select and work on, I began by "creating my life backwards on purpose." While it may sound a little crazy, the concept is really quite simple. First, you imagine yourself achieving all that you set out to achieve and vividly picture what that life would look like in detail. This was a skill I was slowly beginning to master with my new, more open, less cluttered mind.

I started, slowly, to imagine my dream life—that ultimate, ideal life situation. I knew the more detailed I could get, the stronger and clearer my whys would become.

It was time to get down to the nitty-gritty and get laser focused. How many people did I envision in my family? What friends and relatives did I imagine in my sacred "inner circle"? Who would I be spending most of my time with? What would we be doing? What kind of work did I want to be doing? How much time would I be devoting to my career and how much of my precious time would be spent with those I love? What would my typical work day look like? Where would I be living?

The list went on and on. As I answered each question, another question would pop up. The ideas started to flow. Dare I say I was even starting to have some fun imagining this crazy far-off dream life?

I knew my next task would be to work my way backwards to find the steps it would take to achieve this life. But suddenly my old perfect and skeptical self showed up. You see, there was a huge gap between where I was today and where I envisioned myself in this "dream life" scenario. Was this all too much? Were my new dreams too big to actually achieve?

I suddenly realized that if there wasn't a big gap between these two worlds, I wouldn't be thinking big enough. No, this time it wasn't my dreams that needed to get smaller; it was my mind that needed to get bigger, much bigger and much more open to thinking beyond the easy, current scenario that kept me stuck and unhappy.

I reminded myself that the mind is programmed to seek out answers, so the bigger the challenge we present our minds with, the harder it will work to find solutions to answer these challenges. This was the time I needed to stretch my imagination, have some fun, and let my mind work to catch up and get with the program. This was my one and only life I was creating, and I was going to make sure it was big enough to fit this new and improved me.

Now, depending on whether or not you're a fan of the self-help genre, many of the ideas above may sound hauntingly familiar. After all, I never claimed to be the creator of turning dreams into reality. I'm merely a student of the game, here to share my personal experiences and hopefully start your mind on a life-long journey to create YOUR own unique, high-quality life. If you've heard this all before, I'm okay with that, and I'll tell you why.

One important marketing concept I've learned over the years is that people need to hear an idea 7 to 10 times before it actually becomes engraved in their brains. So if this information is not new to you—congratulations. You're one step closer to putting these ideas into your mental database.

On the other hand, if everything I'm talking about is completely new and fresh for you, that is awesome; congratulations—you've just begun an amazing journey to creating the life you've imagined, and I'm excited to continue on with you as you grow and expand these ideas.

With my new dream life floating in my head, I knew I was still missing an important piece if any of this new plan was going to be attainable. I was going to need to take ownership of these ideas and start taking real, tangible action steps every day if I wanted these ideas to actually turn into my future reality.

Whenever you set a goal, it is vitally important to take an immediate action, no matter how big or small, towards that goal. This follows the idea that objects in motion tend to stay in motion. In this case, I not only wanted to stay in motion; I wanted to continue building momentum that would quickly carry me to new levels in my life that I never imagined possible.

I acknowledged that this was a marathon, not a sprint, and that there'd be lots of unexpected twists and turns along the way. But it was a start.

Each small action step reminded me of my power to move my life forward. I reminded myself to start celebrating the little victories—something the old me would never have allowed myself the time to do.

I could feel changes happening inside of me, but I knew this was just the beginning. There was so much to learn and so much to discover. But would I be strong enough and brave enough to continue?

"If you own this story, you get to write the ending."

- Brene Brown

3

THE ART OF
CONSCIOUS CHOICES

"The bad news is time flies.
The good news is you're the pilot."
Michael Attshuler

With my strong whys in place and a set of goals to achieve, I was quickly faced with my next obstacle: lack of time. All of these dreams and plans sounded exciting and promising, but then reality set in. I'm a busy, active adult with lots of people counting on me and lots of things to accomplish each day. I knew I needed to stay organized. I needed a way to manage my time; I needed a system. So, I asked around and observed my friends.

Some used fancy, structured day planners filled with page after page of dated, color-coded, lined columns demanding long, involved entries and plans. Nah, not my style.

Others had a simple calendar on the wall filled with an endless array of scribbles of all the family's activities. Some were even color-coded for each family member. While it may work great for some, when I looked at that calendar, I was instantly stressed-out. Each scribble, to me, symbolized yet another obligation requiring my attention in a never-ending rainbow swirl that left me wondering how to possibly accomplish it all. No thank you.

There were even a wide array of computer programs with flashing buttons, lots of columns, colors, and sorting options designed to create the "perfect calendar for you." It sounded like a full-time job to design and keep it updated. Ummm, pass.

And then I found a few people who completely rebelled against any kind of written lists or systems at all. Yet somehow they still reported experiencing those sleepless nights wrestling with the to-do list stored in their brains, struggling to keep up with each day.

So after exploring the options, even though I'm a big fan of technology, I personally opted for a simple handwritten to-do list. It seemed innocent enough, even sensible and useful. I remembered reading years ago that by keeping a pad of paper and pen next to the bed to scribble your thoughts, you could jot down your list, clear your mind, and even sleep better. Sounded like a plan. What could go wrong?

So here's how it went: At first, things started off quite innocently with a single column on paper. Not so bad. Maybe this could be the answer I needed. However, that list soon expanded and was divided into work and personal lists. Not long later, each of my lists became further divided into things to do, calls to make, and things to get.

While on the surface this whole system appeared to be an organized, sensible way to plot my day and activities, I had a sinking feeling that in my attempt to be organized and ultra-productive, I was seriously losing my way. My list, like my life, was quickly morphing out of control with too many paths, responsibilities and endless chores with no focus.

I was so tied to my lists that if I found myself doing a task that wasn't currently on my list, I would quickly add it just to experience the satisfaction of checking it off moments later.

My list quickly became a huge source of stress for me. It was a constant visual reminder of my perceived inadequacies. Each day, as I scanned this list, I could hear the voices in my head telling me that no matter how hard I tried, and how many hours I put in, my efforts were futile. I wasn't good enough. I would never make any real progress. The list continued to expand, and my stress level continued to increase proportionately.

But it was systematic. It was organized. It had structure and all the fundamentals I had learned. So why wasn't it working?

The reality was that my to-do list was not the problem at all. My issue, it turned out, was that my whole underlying concept of "time management" was flawed, and it was keeping me running in circles in a perpetually imperfect state of stress and failure.

Then it hit me: there was no such thing, at least in my world, as time management. That whole concept was, in my opinion, an ancient myth designed to keep me floundering in a sea of to-do's, making no real progress.

I knew I needed to break this unhealthy cycle and find a new system, but how? No matter what I did and how many late nights I worked, I still had the same 24 hours each day. Time itself could not truly be managed. Instead of finding a better time management system, I realized I needed to find a better way to live. I needed to manage the activities I deemed important, but with a whole new outlook and framework. I needed to make better choices of how to spend my time.

My to-do list represented my time, and similar to my dreams, I had slowly and without noticing given up on actively and intentionally choosing what I did with my time. Instead, I had gotten on an endless cycle of unsuccessfully trying to do more and be more, even when I had no more to give. This cycle had left me feeling defeated, overwhelmed and exhausted.

All these negative emotions further stifled my ability to be productive, and this lack of productivity only intensified all those negative emotions. I was suffering from a bad case of UCM: *Unconscious Choice Management*.

32

In my well-meaning attempt to try to please everyone, I always said yes when asked, even if it meant completely neglecting activities and events that were important to me personally. My health suffered, my energy dipped, and my mood reflected this continual negative mix of struggling and feeling like I was failing daily.

At the same time, it quickly became overwhelmingly clear to me that if I wanted to upscale the quality of my life, then reclaiming my time was a vital step in becoming the person I wanted to become. And so at first—as I often do when faced with a big scary decision—I completely panicked, then I attempted to calm my emotions and think logically, then I argued internally, and finally, I closed my eyes, took a deep breath, and jumped with both feet!

Knowing that the only person on the planet I could actually control was me, I took a hard look at my typical responses to situations to try to figure out what needed to change in me to make this new belief system work. I realized that whenever someone asked me to help with something, even when it was something I had absolutely no time to fit into my schedule, my typical, almost automatic, reaction was, "I'll find time." Looking back, that answer was the key to my struggle AND the key to my solution too.

I wasn't going to "find time." There was no big bag of time to pull from and to add to my day. Instead, I was going to have to sacrifice some other activity to "find time" for the task I'd just agreed to complete. It wasn't more time that I needed. What I really needed was to start making better choices.

There it was! I needed to give up my struggle with time management, and instead, create a whole new system based on CHOICE management. If I could learn to make more conscious choices, then I could finally "find the time" for the truly important things in my life.

With my new choice management system firmly planted in my brain, I soon realized that in order to make the choices that matter, I was going to have to learn another important, and for me, very challenging skill: how to say no.

For some of you, this may be something you've learned long ago, and if that's the case, then congratulations—you are way ahead of me in the game. If, however, like me, you tend to be the person people can always rely on to say yes, then I can tell you right now that this shift in ideas will be a challenging time for you up front, but it will ultimately be a game changer for you, your family, and your life ahead.

Trading in UCM (Unconscious Choice Management)

Every day, practically every minute, whether we do it consciously or not, we are making choices. Ironically, while I was so desperately trying to avoid making bad choices, my indecisiveness was actually the worst choice of all.

"When you need to make a hard decision, flip a coin. Why? Because when that coin is in the air, you suddenly know what you're hoping for." - Unknown

Let me give you an example. I got a business invite from a colleague to attend an evening networking event. Even though I'd been putting in a lot of extra time at work recently and hadn't been home nearly as much as I'd like, my calendar wasn't officially filled that particular night, so I accepted without giving it a second thought. But as the date approached, I began to experience feelings I couldn't quite put my finger on. My stress level increased, my anxiety level rose, and I suddenly started to feel resentful about the invite and wondered why I had said yes in the first place.

So what happened? I was unknowingly experiencing the negative consequences of UCM. You see, while on the surface my answer seemed simple and straightforward, I had actually made a very important choice without even realizing it. In this case, I had chosen work over time with my family along with some much-needed downtime. I was regretting that decision and angry at my environment, and more importantly at myself for not recognizing and weighing that choice more carefully.

"I am not a product of my circumstances. I am a product of my decisions." - Stephen Covey

I had spent so much of my energy trying to find ways to say yes and not disappoint others. In many of those pivotal moments, I was unknowingly saying no to other very important, and often overlooked, parts of my life: my kids, my spouse, my health, and my financial well-being. All this was in jeopardy just because I chose to say an unenthusiastic yes without truly considering my decision fully.

So how would I combat this problem? Would I be forced to just start refusing business invites even if it sabotaged my career? Should I automatically and

34

systematically turn my back on those who asked for my assistance? Of course not! But what I could start doing right away was being more conscious and intentional with my choices and decisions. But to make that happen, there was another equally important concept I was going to have to carefully evaluate: the idea of work/life balance.

Letting Go of the Work/Life Balance Myth

A myth? I had spent most of my adult life desperately struggling to find and maintain the ideal work/life balance. It was a concept I cherished and clung to as the ultimate (yet unattainable) achievement.

In my never-ending attempt to do it all and be everything to everyone, I prided myself on my daily ability to shift, maneuver, and balance my roles of daughter, sister, mother, wife, friend, caregiver, businesswoman…the list went on and on. I was convinced it was not only possible but imperative to find and constantly live a perfectly compartmentalized, orderly life giving complete and equal time to both my career and my family.

Looking back, I realized that not only did I cause myself years of unnecessary stress and pain, but I also may have, again without meaning to, caused those around me unnecessary stress. I had inadvertently helped perpetuate the work/life balance myth by appearing in public (or perhaps only in my own warped mind) to have somehow achieved this sought-after (and mythical) balance.

Ha! What a joke. While my outward egotistical persona worked 24/7 to keep up this facade, internally, I was in constant turmoil and couldn't understand why.

And then it happened. The pressure was too intense. The stress was too much. I finally chose to give up my ego and just admit to myself (even though I'm pretty sure everyone around me had known it for years) that my life was not now nor would it ever be a perfectly balanced symphony.

Instead, my life was one big, long, never-ending juggling act. Yes, a juggling act—that sounds about right. Dozens of invisible balls (priorities, responsibilities, requests) flew through the air above me as I somewhat helplessly looked up trying to plan and react to the ones closest to the ground while at the same time, silently calculating how long I had until the next one hit the floor.

Coming to terms with this image was not easy, but when I finally let go of the work/life myth and embraced my juggling act, I experienced an instant and welcomed sense of peace and relief. No longer faced with the torturous daily chore of maintaining the silly facade of the perfectly balanced life, I was free to explore new ways to channel my time, re-spark my dreams, and reclaim my life.

I realized once again that to move my life forward, I needed to let go of more old ideas that were weighing me down preventing me from being all I wanted to become. I realized I actually had the power to design a whole new set of rules for my life. It was time to get even clearer about what really mattered to me and what was most important moving forward.

However, as I began to face my days with this new set of intentionally created guidelines handy and my whys clear and in focus, I noticed something both amazing and exciting. Suddenly, making those difficult daily decisions became easier and more straightforward because I had a precise and targeted roadmap to follow.

By being more conscious and thoughtful about what I did with each of my precious 24 hours each day, I felt happier and more at ease with my decisions and scheduling. Much of my everyday internal chaos began to fade away. With each day and each conscious, intentional choice, I became stronger, more confident, and more determined to continue on this path to a life I truly loved living. I was starting to choose happy over perfect, and it felt amazing!

"Knowing is not enough. We must APPLY. Willing is not enough. We must DO." - Bruce Lee

As I continued to make more conscious choices, I realized that not only could I make these decisions, but I also had the ability to re-negotiate and adjust these choices at will, taking away that last bit of fear that I'd make the wrong choices.

"It is not about making the right choice. It is about making a choice and making it right." -J. R. Rim

Little did I know that soon my new Choice Management System would be put to the ultimate test.

My Unexpected Choice Management Quiz

It was April 14th, the day before the tax deadline, and my husband Marc and I were both at our office, as we always were, busy cranking out tax returns for clients in our tax and accounting practice. Our young daughter, our only child at the time, had been visiting one set of grandparents and then the other during the last week to allow us time to meet our client deadlines.

A few years earlier, Marc and I had evaluated our business opportunities and had decided it was time to move our home-based business to a local office space. We rented a cute second-story office a few miles from our home and believed we were perfectly poised to live the entrepreneurial life and create a business that allowed us to work side-by-side, provide for our growing family and live comfortably. We were creating the American dream—at least we were in our heads.

However, as I took a quick nap-break on the futon in the office for the third or fourth or fifth night in a row, I looked over at my husband. There he was, sitting at his desk with his air mattress next to him ready for him to take a quick nap in-between client files. I suddenly started to wonder if this was really the life we had imagined.

Being an entrepreneur was the only lifestyle I knew. My dad owned an appliance repair business when I was born, and from the time I could hold a screwdriver, I had watched my parents work hard, put in long hours, and help other people whenever they could. While we certainly weren't rich by any stretch of the imagination, we had a home, a car, and lots of people around us who cared about us. We were comfortable, and we were happy. So now as an adult and as a new parent, why had MY dream gone so terribly wrong?

My husband is a CPA—a logical, methodical thinker who carefully weighs all the pros and cons of any situation before making a decision. I, on the other hand, tend to lead with my emotions and go with my gut. Most of my decisions at that time were fueled by my overwhelming desire to be the best and have it all at any cost. However, in that moment, something clicked, and our two very different decision-making systems united. This was NOT the life we had dreamed of, and the only way to change it was for us to actively and very intentionally change it ourselves, now.

We finished up our client files, met our client deadlines, and immediately started searching for the right person or people to take over our practice. After making the needed arrangements to be sure that everyone would be taken care of, we said farewell to our accounting practice, moved back into our home office, and started planning what our next move would be in this unknown next chapter.

Was it scary? Oh yes! Was it necessary? Oh, heck yes! Guided by our whys, many of the previously grey areas became instantly black and white. With our new Conscious Choice System engraved in our minds, although this decision was HUGE for us, there truly was no other option or choice.

"The only thing scarier than change is regret."

–Unknown

4

PROGRESS THROUGH ACCOUNTABILITY

*"The moment you take responsibility
for everything in your life is the moment you can change anything in
your life."*
Hal Elrod

"If I could just lose 15 pounds…"
"If I could just be like my friends and go to the gym every day…"
"If I could just have more willpower with my diet…"

If you can relate to any of the phrases above, then I hope you will still respect me when I confess: Hi, my name is Wendy, and I was a serial exercise quitter. It's not something I'm proud of, but it was definitely something I had resigned myself to accept.

Now you may be asking yourself, "What exactly IS a serial exercise quitter?" Great question! Let me give you a little personal context for the term. I would walk by my family watching a television show and hear the fitness infomercials advertising the latest, greatest exercise DVD program on the market. It would sound amazing!

And while I knew I would never have the body of the women in the commercial, some tangible results seemed attainable. All you need is 30 minutes a day. Just put on the boxing gloves and watch the pounds melt away. Eat real food 6 times a day and have the body of your dreams.

As someone who gets easily bored and distracted and likes to succeed in everything I attempt, I was always looking for the next quick-fix program to get the health results I had imagined. I was intrigued by new gadgets and ideas and always anxious to see what new technology and innovation could offer me. All of that would have been fine, if I ever lasted past week two of trying any of the gadgets and programs I purchased!

So here's how the typical scenario would play out for me over and over again. First, my package would arrive, and I would excitedly open the DVD and immediately start the workout. Not so bad. Feeling great. This enthusiasm and dedication to the new routine would usually continue for about 4 to 10 days— 2 weeks max!

After that time, a very predictable cycle would kick in. I would wake up one day and not feel quite myself - a little sore here, and a little tired there. All "valid" reasons (at least in my head) to skip a workout. And yes, those feelings would continue the next day, and the next day, and before I knew it, I no longer had any sort of exercise routine.

But that was okay, because in another month or two, I would see another amazing program, and for "only $19.95 plus shipping and handling," I would begin this whole useless and ineffective cycle again. The craziest part is that it became such a normal part of my life that it never even dawned on me that I was setting myself up to fail time after time.

I'm guessing you may be thinking of someone in your life who exhibits similar behavior in some aspect, and if you don't know anyone like this, either you're hanging with an awesome crowd OR that someone might be you!

Ironically, even though I consider myself to be a relatively intelligent human being with some level of self-awareness, it actually took an off-hand comment from one of my kids to finally shake me out of this cycle of denial.

I had gotten a new set of DVDs, and as usual, I was excited to get started. My daughter was in her room, and when I passed by her door, I couldn't help but tell her about this amazing new program I was about to start and all of the amazing results I was looking forward to achieving.

My kids are usually incredibly supportive, so I guess that's why I was so taken aback when my daughter replied in a rather skeptical (even sarcastic) tone, "Uh-huh. Ok, Mom. Sure. See you in a week."

I was in a momentary state of shock. Could it actually be that my daughter was doubting me? Had I not shown her by example time and time again that anything is possible with the right plan, attitude, and focus? It was in that moment that I was forced to face a painful reality about my own behavior. I realized my daughter had every reason to be skeptical.

Her past experience had shown her that when it came to Mom taking care of everyone else, I could be relied on to follow through and get the job done. But when it came to me taking care of myself, she had repeatedly witnessed me stuck in a wasteful cycle that produced no real results and no long-term changes or new habits.

So now I understood her reaction and even learned something new about myself, but I still had absolutely no clue what was behind my total lack of success in this area of my life, and more importantly, how I could begin to fix it.

As I looked at other areas of my life—my business, my family, my children, and my community causes—I was baffled by my lack of results in the health and wellness area of my life.

If my kids had a problem or needed something, I did whatever it took to help them find a solution. If I had a goal I wanted to achieve in my business, I set up plans, found the necessary resources, and made it work. If someone reached out to me with a worthy cause that I wanted to support and felt passionate about, no matter what the roadblocks, I made things happen. So why wasn't I able to do this with my own health?

I had to face yet another harsh realization: I didn't value my own health nearly as much as the plights and needs of those around me. Although I publicly professed time after time how important it was to be healthy in order to achieve all that you want in your life, my words were hollow, and this concept was one I had never fully embraced and owned.

Ok, so now I knew the root of the problem, but I was still miles away from any possible plan or solution to move myself forward. I was stuck again. But, as I was starting to realize more and more, the answers I need were usually right in plain sight if I opened up my stubborn mind enough to look.

Why Does a Millionaire Need a Coach?

A few weeks later, I was reading a book, *First Steps to Wealth*, by multi-millionaire Dani Johnson. She was talking about a conversation she had with her business coach. I was confused. At this point in her story, Dani, after experiencing a horrific childhood, then earning and losing millions in her personal journey, was a multimillionaire. A business coach? Really? I thought by the time you had reached that level of success, you'd already know what you need to do to succeed. Why would she need a coach?

She went on to discuss the incredible value she found in having someone holding her continuously accountable for her actions and goals. An accountability partner? Hmmm…interesting idea.

While sometimes things sneak up on you slowly and unnoticed, this time a single moment just hit me and suddenly changed everything.

In all the other aspects of my life, I would freely share my goals, dreams and needs with everyone in an attempt to find the answers and resources required to succeed. But when it came to my own health and fitness plans, I remained silent and alone. I presumed inevitable failure from the start, and I didn't want to expose that flaw and weakness to the world.

Armed with this newfound understanding, I was determined to break this unhealthy and unproductive cycle. Was I scared? Heck yeah. Did I do it anyway? Again, heck yeah. I was learning that big rewards take big actions and often big risks. Without my continued good health, the rest was meaningless. I had to make this change no matter how fearful and uncomfortable I currently felt.

I decided to tackle a 10-week exercise DVD series. I also simultaneously decided, for the first time ever, that I was going to put my goal out there in the harsh, bright public light. For the first time ever in my life, and I was going to find a way to succeed in this area of my life and make it through all 10 weeks to complete this program.

I had a Facebook friend, Tara Davis, who was a health coach. From her posts online, she appeared to be a fellow busy mom who shared my challenges of trying to juggle it all. But, at least in the health and wellness side, there seemed to be a noticeable difference between us. She seemed to have figured out how to put her health towards the top of the list—a skill I desperately needed to learn.

From the little bit I personally knew about her, she seemed approachable and caring, so I swallowed my pride, put my ego aside, typed her a Facebook message, and actually hit SEND. She quickly responded and shared that she had an accountability group forming on Facebook.

A Facebook group, huh? That sounded do-able. No face-to-face interaction, somewhat anonymous, easy to blend in (and fade away if necessary). All my old insecurities and doubts liked this idea, but would it be possible for this group to actually make the difference I needed to break through this lifelong cycle? Was I really looking to be accountable or was this just another easy way out?

"If you really want to do something, you'll find a way; if you don't, you'll find an excuse."

- Jim Rohn

Lucky for me, my new coach understood more than I realized about being accountable, and she was ready, willing, and able to see right through my hesitation and keep me on track. Besides the support of the Facebook group, she would periodically message me and even call me on the phone to make sure that I was doing okay and to see if I needed any additional encouragement (or a little kick in the pants) to keep me moving forward towards my goal.

My exercise goals became her goals too, and she helped me refocus whenever I momentarily got off track. She also helped me acknowledge and celebrate my little victories along the way.

Suddenly, I knew I had discovered the "secret sauce" to moving this goal forward. This time things were different. I would not fail in public, and I would not let my coach, Tara, down. More importantly, I began to realize I wouldn't let ME down!

I'm proud to say I completed the 10-week program, and I even filled out the optional info survey online to get my reward for finishing the program: a t-shirt. I wore that silly t-shirt as a badge of honor. I STILL do, and I'm happy to report that it fits me much better now too. This simple little shirt was my trophy of completion. I was no longer a quitter in the exercise arena.

If the story ended there, everything would have been great—a storybook ending. Set Goal - Accomplish Goal - Success! But again, while my outward appearance was successful and triumphant, inwardly, I was still skeptical, still questioning my own abilities and willpower, battling years of multiple fitness failures.

As happy as I was the day I had completed that program, I hadn't adequately prepared myself for the days to follow. My brain heard "completed," checked exercise off the list, and within days I fell right back into my old unproductive, self-sabotaging ways.

However, something was different this time. Something substantial had changed. I had resources. I had accountability. I had my Facebook community and my coach. Did I feel momentarily defeated? Yes. Did I now have the tools and support to refocus and start again? Absolutely!

Although it took me quite a while to pick myself up and begin again, this time I knew success was possible. I had gotten a taste of what it felt like to finally achieve in this area of my life, and that, along with the support system I had developed, allowed me to come back stronger and with even more resolve. And although I can't proclaim to be the world's most consistent exerciser, I now have the skillset and mental tools to continue to grow in this area, even when those minor setbacks happen.

As an added side note, I continued to stay in touch with my coach Tara, and a few months later, Tara posted that Dani Johnson (the guru who had indirectly started me off on this leg of my journey) was coming to Baltimore. We attended this amazing weekend event together, and that decision, once again, change the course of my journey.

5

TURNING THE PROFESSOR INTO THE STUDENT

*"We have two ears and one mouth so t
hat we can listen twice as much as we speak."*

Epictetus

I've spent most of my adult life creating, running, or helping grow small businesses. I've been blessed to have the opportunity to formally and informally mentor many talented businesswomen and men. I've always loved sharing my ideas and knowledge to help others excel in both their professional and personal lives.

Up until this point, I had considered myself to be a pretty open- minded, good listener. Ironically, and unbeknownst to me at the time, while I was working so hard to help others identify their strengths and weaknesses in order for them to succeed, I was completely oblivious to my own potentially fatal flaws.

As I continued reading Dani Johnson's book, *First Steps to Wealth*, she shared a story about a potential business mentor who agreed to guide and teach her under a few very specific conditions. One of these conditions was that she follow directions. She needed to prove she was teachable.

As I read this, I couldn't help but think…aren't we all teachable given the right teacher? How silly. But as I began to think more about this, I started to realize that perhaps it wasn't silly at all. In fact, perhaps in the middle of trying to always be the perfect, helpful mentor and guide, I had lost the critically important ability to put my own ego-filled, know-it-all self aside and really listen and learn from those around me.

Perhaps this experience is something you can relate to or maybe it's completely foreign and far removed from your personal situation, but here's a few questions I was forced to ask myself, and perhaps you may want to consider them too.

In a group setting, when a topic comes up (even if it's a topic you know very little about), do you tend to immediately feel like you have all the answers or at least more than anyone else at the table?

When someone suggests or proposes a solution, do you tend to immediately begin adding ideas of how to improve upon the idea, even before you've actually taken a moment to consider the idea itself?

During a typical conversation in your day, when the other person is speaking, are you actually listening to what they're saying or are you busy working on creating your reply?

Depending on your answers to the questions above, you may discover, as I did, that learning to be teachable may not be such a farfetched idea after all.

Regaining this skill, while initially painful, was really quite a simple process once I accepted one obvious and vital life lesson: I don't know everything.

Yup, it was really that simple and yet that complicated all at the same time. After so many years of internally believing, and externally teaching, all the lessons I had learned and knowledge I had gained, I was still missing so much! Everyone I encountered throughout my day had so much to share and teach me.

As I slowly let down my self-imposed set of blinders and gave up my need to always be right, new and exciting ideas and information came rushing at me at a high rate of speed. I began learning new skills, gaining amazing tidbits of knowledge in every conversation and fully appreciating (and showing gratitude) to the many people I came into contact with on a daily basis.

Putting My Teachability to the Test

Now that I had decided deep down in my being that I was going to become teachable, a brand new fear crept in: Could I actually learn?

Looking back on my myriad of business ventures, I realized I had created and designed each opportunity using a similar pattern and process. With each new business, I would identify a skill I already had and felt comfortable with, and then I would create a business around that skill. But when I decided to take on a new and different opportunity, I knew this comfortable, predictable pattern was about to be turned upside-down.

"If someone offers you an amazing opportunity and you're not sure you can do it, say yes, then learn how to do it later." -Richard Branson

After a brief time as the marketing coordinator for a mortgage company, I had decided to take the leap and become a full-time loan officer. I was breaking out of my usual mold, deciding to go after this opportunity, committed to learning the required skillset along the way. It was my own version of "on the job training," and it was going to test my teachability in every possible way.

Lucky for me, I had developed a pretty strong set of test-taking skills over the years, and I quickly passed the required licensing exam. That was great. That was exciting. I had experienced a little moment of success in my new journey.

However, it didn't take long for me to realize that there was a huge difference between passing a test and actually being an everyday, real life, functional, useful, homeowner-creating loan officer.

"If we wait until we're ready, we'll be waiting for the rest of our lives." - Lemony Snicket

I knew I was going to need to draw on all the lessons I had learned so far in my "recreating a happy me" adventure, but it didn't take long for those old fears and doubts to start creeping in.

After so many years, did I have what it would take to start something new again? While I was confident in my abilities to market myself and connect and help other people through the mortgage process, a huge nagging set of questions lingered in my brain.

53

Were my whys strong enough for this new endeavor? Was my ego truly tucked away to allow me to accept myself as a newbie? For the foreseeable future, I was going to have to lay down my comfortable, lifelong role of mentor, and try on a brand new, pretty odd feeling and uncomfortable role: mentee.

"If you're not willing to learn, no one can help you. If you're determined to learn, no one can stop you." -Zig Ziglar

To be successful in this new career, I needed to open my mind, be vulnerable (a life skill I had not had much practice at), and reach out to my mentors, humbly requesting help and guidance as I began this new business role.

This time, I would be the student, not the teacher. I would need to put every last ounce of my newly learned teachable skills into play if I had any chance of making this work. It was time to put all the lessons into action, swallow my useless pride, keep my mouth shut (or at least TRY to), quiet my overactive mind, and just listen and learn.

I asked myself, "What's the worst possible outcome if I take the step and try?" And much more importantly, I asked myself, "What's the worst possible outcome if I don't?"

How will I feel five years from now if I'm still in the same place I am today? Stuck? Overwhelmed? Unhappy? Unfulfilled? Am I willing to accept that? Decision made. I would become the best possible loan officer I could be, helping as many people as I could along the way.

At my desk, I hung up a copy of my company's tagline, adding even more strong whys to my list: "Inspiring Hope. Delivering Dreams. Building Prosperity."

"When you step out of your comfort zone, you are stepping into your greatness." - Cynthia Chiam

I cautiously and timidly took that step yet again out of my comfort zone and into a wild new world feeling weak, exposed, and quite vulnerable. Ironically, looking back on it now, I realize that the moment I perceived myself as weak was actually one of the bravest moments in my whole life. I allowed myself to utilize all of my newfound skills and leave my self-important, useless ego behind. I was ready to go all in.

In the weeks and months that followed, I continued to focus on closing my mouth and opening my ears to take full advantage of all the knowledge and guidance my mentors had to share. While I know I pushed their patience to the brink on more than one occasion (and still sometimes do!), slowly I began to accept that sometimes when I asked a question, it was ok to just hear the answer without immediately putting in my two cents—a skill I'm still very much working on mastering!

Now don't get me wrong. I'm certainly not saying that I blindly accept everything I'm told without ever questioning or disagreeing. But now (at least most of the time) when I speak up, I actually take time to process the comments and consider my thoughts before they come flying off my tongue.

It was definitely an uncertain, uncomfortable, unfamiliar time for me, letting go of being the one always in charge and instead, being open to truly listen and learn again. I knew there would be many struggles and obstacles along the way, both external and internal, but I also knew this was a pivotal moment in my career, and much more importantly in my life's journey to create the new and improved version of myself that I had vowed to develop.

"If you don't go after what you want, you'll never have it. If you don't ask, the answer is always no. If you don't step forward, you're always in the same place." - Nora Roberts

My takeaway from this experience? If you really want something after carefully considering the opportunity at hand, take a deep breath, set your ego aside, and JUMP with both feet! But first, make sure you've created a soft foundation to land on, carefully selecting and surrounding yourself with a strong inner circle.

"In the end, we only regret the chances we didn't take, relationships we were afraid to have and the decisions we waited too long to make." - Lewis Carroll

For me, having this personal support and having business teammates and mentors who were generous with their knowledge, patient, and ready to provide the relatively safe landing I needed made this leap of faith all worthwhile.

Maybe you've found yourself at a similar professional or personal crossroads, wondering if you have what it takes to make the next step. Perhaps it's a promotion that's been in the back of your mind, but you hesitated to take that next step and apply. Maybe it's a coworker you've always imagined could help guide and lead you to the next level in your career, but you hesitated to open yourself up to approaching them for fear of his or her possible response or out of concern for being looked down upon for asking.

Maybe you've always wanted to play the guitar, learn to cook, ride a motorcycle, etc. Find someone who has the skill you desire, and seek out the mentors you need to move forward. Take the leap!

6

HARNESSING THE POWER OF FEAR TO MOVE FORWARD

"Too many of us are not living our dreams because we are living our fears."

Les Brown

When I first started to write this chapter, it was going to be titled "Fearless." But then I realized that fearless means having no fear at all. And if you're anything at all like me, you experience fear at some point throughout your daily life—maybe even multiple times throughout each day! It seems to be an inevitable part of our existence, so I decided to start by accepting that if I was ever going to step out of my comfort zone, even taking baby steps, then being fearless was virtually impossible.

So right about now you may be thinking, "Well, this is great—I've just been informed that I'm destined to live in fear my entire life," and while yes, that is part of what I'm saying, the uplifting and exciting second part of that realization is that while fear may be inevitable, how we choose to react and use that fear makes all the difference. We are 100% in control of our responses and reactions.

"Courage is not the absence of fear, but rather the assessment that something else is more important than fear." - Franklin D. Roosevelt

I realized the decision was mine: I could either wallow in my fear and let it paralyze me, bringing my plans and dreams to a screeching halt, OR I could embrace that fear and use its power and energy to help me get laser-focused on my ultimate plans, allowing myself to rocket through the fear to my dreams on the other side.

While intellectually, I knew that all sounded like a great plan, mentally and emotionally, I also knew if I had any chance of walking through my fears, I was going to need to make some serious adjustments to my mindset.

I've personally lived through more than a few periods where I had to decide how much power I was going to give fear, but one time in particular jumps to my mind.

Several years ago, my husband suffered a completely unexpected and quite dramatic heart attack. (Spoiler alert: He's doing great now!) Without putting you through the gory details, that the particular artery (aka the "widow maker" artery) and situation he encountered had a 10% survival rate. These are not odds I would wish on anyone.

We started the long and challenging recovery period. I say "we" because I strongly believe that when a loved one goes through a life-threatening medical emergency, the family, as well as the patient, must travel through a healing and recovery cycle.

Was I afraid? I was scared beyond any words I could ever use to even describe my level of fear. Did I have choices? Well, some would say no, but I would disagree. The situation was what it was, but I still had the choice of how I was going to react and proceed based on this new situation.

Of course I clearly and immediately saw the "easy and expected" option: I could give up, give in, and break down. I must admit I strongly considered that choice on a number of occasions throughout those first few months. However, there was another option: Choice #2.

This option would require me to fight through the fear daily (or sometimes hourly) and keep my mind focused on the positive. I had to constantly remind myself, sometimes minute by minute, that how I chose to view my reality was completely my choice and completely in my control (even though there was very little else I could even begin to control at this point).

I had a husband I loved who needed his wife's support, and I had three young daughters who needed their mom. Decision made: Keep moving through the fear!

Hopefully the fears you face daily are not the life-threatening variety, but I've come to realize that the same life survival skills required to conquer and face fear in crisis are the very same skills we can apply to meet and conquer our everyday fears in our careers and relationships and within our own mind.

The Two Innate Fears

I recently heard a discussion that suggested that humans are born with only two innate fears:

1. the fear of falling
2. the fear of loud noises

Now if you're into scientific research or if you are a former school debate team member, I'm sure this statement could open up hours of lively conversation.

However, since I'm neither of these, I was personally struck by the idea that if these truly are the only two fears we are born with, then all the rest of the long laundry list of things we struggle with and fear each day are either learned or self-created. Hold on! If that is true, then it seems possible to unlearn or even ignore those invisible demons that had been standing in my way.

Armed with this amazing new revelation, I began examining my own fears that I'd allowed to consciously and unconsciously slow me down or even stop me from pursuing my dreams and accomplishing my goals. I encourage you to take a moment to think about the fears, big and small, that are standing between you and the life you imagine and deserve.

As I mentioned earlier when I discussed my exercise journey, one of my big fears that I was finally forced to recognize and face head-on was my fear of failing in public. The crazy part was that after all these years, I still had not been able to identify and put a name to that fear, making it impossible for me to acknowledge and conquer it.

I started reminding myself daily that this fear was NOT reality, and I could move beyond it. I stopped focusing on the fear and instead started thinking about what it would actually be like if I moved beyond this fear. What would that look like? What would it feel like to remove that self-imposed glass ceiling? What would it take to make that happen? What would need to change in me?

Once I was finally able to identify and put a name to that fear, I began to clearly see an incredible pattern that had totally escaped me before.

As my mindset shifted and this pattern emerged, I began to more easily form and focus clear and attainable goals. This led me to start questioning what other underground fears were lurking inside of me that were unknowingly holding me back from being the best me I could be and enjoying my life to the fullest.

Now for you, the fears standing in your way may be clear and straightforward: fear of public speaking, fear of confrontation, fear of embarrassing yourself in front of others, and the list goes on and on. Putting a name to these fears became my first big step in developing a plan to work through these fears and to create the life I'd imagined. But again, when faced with a question that seems so straightforward on the surface, I was stumped.

Outwardly, I didn't think I was afraid of anything consequential, and yet I knew something was holding me back. I was going to need to dig deeper and really take a brutally honest look at myself if I was going to move forward. I soon discovered that for me, my deepest fears were often most closely linked to times I felt that I had failed or fallen short of what I expected of myself.

I realized that by thinking about times I hadn't lived up to my own high expectations, I could start to see trends or themes emerge that might lead me closer to the breakthrough I needed to move forward.

I began a rather painful but necessary exercise of scribbling down a random list of times I felt afraid. Now, I'm not talking about the fear you feel when you see creepy crawling bugs nearby or hear an unexplained noise at night. I'm talking about uncovering fears that are literally holding your life hostage, maybe without you even knowing it!

Since I had been an entrepreneur for most of my adult life, it made sense to me that the fears I had identified so far mostly involved what I perceived as my public image. I began to think back on the businesses I had created. While most of the businesses I had been involved in had reached some level of success, and brought me pride and smiles when I recalled them, I also began to realize that these business choices and actions might hold important clues in my fear-seeking journey.

In most cases, the businesses I created involved me vaguely identifying a skill I thought I had, then coming up with an idea (some better than others) of how to use that skill to make money, and then putting that idea into action. That part seemed a logical path to follow, but what happened next in most of those businesses suddenly jumped out at me.

For the most part, after reaching a certain safe and respectable level of success (at least in my own mind), I would become distracted and restless and move on to the next big idea.

While I had always attributed this restlessness to my entrepreneurial spirit, I began to realize there was also another quieter, more insidious layer of reasoning that was unconsciously steering many of my actions and choices.

I had developed a fear of not being good enough to propel and excel to the next level. I had quite unknowingly created my own glass ceiling, predetermining the maximum level of success I could imagine as possible and then creating a self-fulfilling prophecy by never going above that level. I had inadvertently developed a fear of thinking big. I was actually afraid to succeed in a really big way.

> **"Our deepest fear is not that we are inadequate. Our deepest fear is that we are powerful beyond measure. It is our light, not our darkness that most frightens us. We ask ourselves, 'Who am I to be brilliant, gorgeous, talented, fabulous?' Actually, who are you not to be?" - Marianne Williamson**

As I struggled to understand and come to terms with this newly discovered dimension of my mindset, the pieces began to come together, and I stumbled across another possible root of this limiting belief: I was a people pleaser. While this was a big plus in some ways, allowing me to connect with people easily, enjoy the work I was doing, and impact my little piece of the world, it was also a potentially fatal flaw.

Each time I started to grow and experience some level of success, I was keenly aware that as my success increased, there would be some around me who began to grow bitter and resentful of my newfound success and happiness. Based on these mounting past experiences, and my perceived view of my own world, I had unconsciously put limits on my ability to thrive beyond a particular point.

I looked around me and saw others struggling, and I wrongly convinced myself that limiting my own success would somehow elevate them, or at least lessen their pain. If only I had realized then that by allowing myself to experience success and reap the benefits of that hard work, it would have allowed me an even greater ability to help and lift up those around me.

> **"They say misery loves company, but so does mediocrity. Don't let the limiting beliefs of OTHERS limit what's possible for YOU."**
> **- Hal Elrod**

I was a young businesswoman with no real-life experience with the daily handling of money matters. That fact combined with my overwhelming desire to always "be there" anytime someone needed financial help, had led me down a very dangerous financial path seriously threatening my ability to move forward.

My confidence in my ability to make sound financial decisions was non-existent, and I was paralyzed with an overwhelming fear of repeating past mistakes. I wanted to be perfect, at least to the outside world, and that created a dual fear: fear of making the wrong decision AND fear that my fatal flaws would be uncovered and exposed publicly at any given moment.

I was a victim of "fake it till you make it" syndrome. While I strongly supported the notion of creating the outside persona you desire and then living that life until your actual life catches up, I had gone so deeply into that phoney life, that I felt powerless to shed that persona and try something new even when the current mask wasn't serving me well anymore.

I realized it was time to make another decision that would dramatically alter my future plans and choices. I had to decide if I was going to continue to live my life as is and settle into the fear like a comfortable old shoe, OR if I was going to take a scary, and almost unimaginable, step out of that zone and be vulnerable. I would have to cast my ego aside once again and give up my perfect public persona (even if it only existed in my own head). It was time to take the chance reaching out to others to try to learn ways to be happy and imperfect at the same time.

"Asking for help when you need it is a sign of strength, not weakness." -Jesse Lyn Stoner

I realized that fear and worry were intimately interrelated, and all the years I spent worrying were keeping me stuck. I desperately needed to get UNstuck. It was time for a major change.

Niyi Sobo, former NFL running back, motivational coach and podcaster at imnotyou.com, discussed fear in an interview. He made a bold and eye-opening comment that led me to another self-discovery.

He said that fear is ego-centered. When you're afraid, you're thinking about yourself and how people will view you or judge you.

The solution: Change your focus to others and to the impact you can have on them, and the fear will go away.

While I still felt powerless to face or overcome my fears, the idea that I could take control and direct my focus was an idea I could relate to and embrace. After all, fear made me feel completely OUT of control—a feeling I did not like at all, so the idea of having ANY sense of control in fearful situations sounded good to me.

"Being uncomfortable is inevitable, so get used to it." - Niyi Sobo

I became even more dedicated to the idea that the easiest and most direct way to propel my dreams forward would be to help others achieve their dreams along the way and to do my best to lift others up along my journey.

"You can have everything in life you want, if you will just help other people get what they want."
- Zig Ziglar

While I liked the idea of taking control, I still felt quite vulnerable when thinking about facing fears and worries, so I knew there had to be more.

Mitch Matthews, author of *Ignite* and host of the Dream, Think, Do podcast, discussed the idea of three buckets of worry:

- Can I control it?
- Can I influence it?
- Do I need to let it go?

To learn more about his ideas, I encourage you to check out his "Punch Worry in the Face" series of podcasts/blog posts.

For me, while the details of his ideas were fantastic and well worth listening to and trying to implement in my everyday life, the big key takeaway I got was that when it came to things I was worried about or afraid of, I needed to break those fears down and decide how to best deal with and conquer each one.

I didn't realize at the time that actually completing and publishing the book you're now reading would put all these new ideas and theories to the ultimate test.

7

TO PUBLISH OR
NOT TO PUBLISH:
THAT IS THE QUESTION

"It always seems impossible until it's done."

Nelson Mandela

When I began to write this book, I was excited, focused, and ready to share my message with the world. But then…as it often happens, fear and worries started to sneak in and undermine my plans.

Those old familiar thought patterns started racing through my brain: Who was I to think I could actually write a whole book? Why would anyone ever want to hear my stories of my life lessons learned?

And even more importantly, why in the world would I ever make the conscious decision to actually gather all my failures into one compact book and put them on display for the world to see?

After all this wonderful search for knowledge and quest to change my mindset and attitudes, I could quickly feel it all crumbling around me as my old mindset, fears and doubts grew bigger and bolder by the minute.

My knee-jerk reaction was to just stop writing and announce as graciously as I possibly could that "due to unforeseen circumstances, I wasn't going to be publishing a book after all." After that, I would do my best to get back to some sort of normalcy, allowing my tattered ego to remain somewhat intact. Yup, that was definitely an option I considered.

But something big had changed inside me. Yes, I was engulfed in a sea of fear, doubt, stress and anxiety, but somewhere mixed in with all of that was this little voice reminding me that I started this project for a purpose: my whys.

Yes, my whys. This was it. It was time to see if I had learned enough in my journey and built strong enough whys to overcome this wave of doubt. Why WAS I doing this after all?

I started with the simplest answer: I wanted to contribute. I wanted to show my readers, through example, that no matter where you are right now in your life, there is hope to make changes if you're willing to give up your ego and take the plunge.

Ha! Yes, ego. My why #2. After all this soul-searching and self-discovery, I was still completely stressed even imagining the idea of not completing a goal I had set out to achieve. Drat my ego! But wait, maybe it wasn't my ego at all. Maybe I actually HAD learned something along the way. Maybe the fear and worry I was experiencing was something different this time and NOT driven by my ego.

If the old me had decided to take on a project like this, there is one thing I know I would absolutely, 100% NOT have done: tell anyone! As I shared earlier, one of my biggest fears, as I had recently discovered, was my fear of failing in public. But even though that fear was by no means gone or even securely tucked away deep in my mind, somehow I had still taken the step out of my comfort zone to announce my book.

Not only had I shared with friends and family that I was writing a book; I had actually publicly announced on social media that my book was underway. I had even posted possible book cover designs on Facebook and asked for feedback. I had even gone a step further and created a short survey about some of my books themes and asked for people to assist me by sharing their thoughts and opinions.

I had certainly made sure that there were plenty of people to hold me accountable to this goal. Hmmm...this was definitely something new for me. But was it enough to keep me moving forward through this latest round of fears and doubts? (Since you're reading my book, I guess you already know the answer, but I hope you'll continue on to hear more about the changes I discovered.)

Ok, so yes, I held myself publicly accountable, which was a step forward. But as exciting as that mini-breakthrough was, I still wasn't sure it was enough to stop me from pulling the plug on this project, giving into years of doubts, fears, and worries about my public image, and continuing on with the status quo.

But that voice in my head—that nagging little sound that didn't seem willing to accept defeat—kept reminding me to think about my whys. As I sat at my desk pondering what my next move would be, I glanced at a picture of my daughters and husband—my ultimate whys for everything I do. They had been with me throughout this book-writing adventure. They had watched me get excited when my first ideas came together, and they had also encouraged me when other ideas wouldn't flow quite the way I had hoped.

But through it all, they believed in me and believed I'd be publishing this book. What kind of an example would I be setting for my girls if I had quit? How would I explain this change of heart to them? More importantly, how could I justify this change in heart to ME!

I realized that as scary as the idea was of putting myself out there in the public's eye, the idea of NOT completing this project was even more frightening. This book was my message to the world, but more importantly, it was my message to my three amazing daughters. One of my strongest desires was to teach and lift my girls up, filling their minds with so much strength, self-esteem and confidence that no one and nothing would stop them from reaching whatever they wanted to achieve in life.

Yes, this was my little notebook to them—my cheat sheet of how to live a happy life and how to hopefully avoid many of the setbacks and disappointments I had experienced because it took me so long to finally start learning and internalizing these lessons.

Wow! These new ideas actually seemed to be sinking in! Decision made: I would walk through the fear.

I quickly called one of my closest friends and told her the struggle I was going through. She immediately started reminding me of how far I had come, and she also reminded me of the impact I wanted to make in the world. By the time I finished talking with her, I realized I'd done a pretty darn good job at choosing my inner circle of inspiring people.

I finally truly began to realize just how powerful asking for help is and how amazing and vitally important it is to create a circle of trusted people in your life who will lift you up when you can't do it alone.

Perhaps I really was teachable after all! All of those lessons I had tried to share through my experiences all seemed to be coming into play in one giant, big, final exam of an experience. I was going to finish my book whether it was a hit or a flop, and I was going to continue to learn how to keep choosing happy, giving up my antiquated ideas about who I needed to be or who I was supposed to be to everyone.

Instead, I was going to continue to create my life intentionally, the good, the bad, and everything in-between. Life wasn't going to be perfect. In fact, it was going to be quite messy and a little out of control on most days, but it was going to be MINE.

8

THE UNIVERSE IS KNOCKING: OPEN THE DOOR!

*"At the moment of commitment,
the universe conspires to assist you."
- Johann Wolfgang von Goethe*

Throughout our lives, there are individual moments and events that change everything. Some are the obvious ones: a marriage proposal; the birth of a child; the death of a loved one; or a cancer diagnosis.

But then there are the others—the NOT so obvious moments that are just as potentially life-altering. They are the little blips on our life's radar screen that will go completely unnoticed and undetected unless we are ultra-aware and actively looking for them. These are the magical, game-changing moments that the universe supplies for us regularly IF we are ready and willing to accept them.

I have to admit that for the first half (or more) of my adult life, I was totally and completely oblivious to these moments. Looking back, I wonder just how many I probably let pass me by. But, I've learned (for the most part) not to dwell in the past anymore. What's done is done. It is what it is. My head is pointed forward in the direction of my dreams.

> **"You can't drive your car looking through the rearview mirror. Life is much like driving; you must be focused on the good things coming your way."** -
> **Shenita Sanders**

The decision to write this book came in one of those moments. I had briefly toyed with the idea of writing a book, but quickly dismissed the idea as a far-fetched fantasy. I was too busy. I had no free time. Besides, what did I really have to share that everyone didn't already know?

How My Broken Cell Phone Led Me to Write

A random issue with my cell phone led me to the local wireless store. I was greeted by a polite young employee (I've noticed as I've gotten older, my definition of "young" has definitely changed). While he was checking out my phone, we began chatting. The conversation turned to him telling me about his current life situation. He had a baby on the way and lots of big dreams for his family, but I could tell he was struggling inside with exactly how he was going to move himself forward into the big life he imagined. He was telling me about his group of friends and how none of them seemed to share his excitement and vision for the future.

In my little everyday world, I was surrounded by encouraging, positive forces, and I naively assumed that was a universal condition. I casually mentioned Jim Rohn's quote, "You are the average of the five people you spend the most time with," thinking this was common knowledge and nothing too noteworthy. So you can imagine my surprise when I saw this young man's eyes light up as he grabbed a piece of paper and asked me to repeat the quote and spell the name of the person who said it.

Still being a bit oblivious to the universe's subtle messages, I didn't think anything of this until we continued to talk. As we did, I realized how excited and interested this gentleman was in learning more about the ideas of reaching beyond your comfort zone to achieve big things. As I mentioned podcasts and a few of my gurus at the time, he couldn't seem to write fast enough, taking notes on practically every word I said.

Suddenly it hit me. Maybe I did have something relevant to share. Maybe I did have something useful to contribute. Maybe the ideas and skills I continued to learn were NOT common knowledge outside of my little world. It was then I made the decision to get serious about actually publishing the book you're now reading. One man and one chance encounter changed my path, because I was listening when the universe started talking.

From a Fundraiser
to a Brand New Career

In another random encounter, I reconnected with a dear friend, Bill Sohan, who was in the mortgage business.

We had met years before through an entrepreneurial networking group. Not long after we had casually met in passing, I was put in charge of a charity fundraiser for our group, and Bill offered to be on my committee. Our group members were amazing and giving business leaders, but they were also very busy people. As the event grew closer, my committee grew smaller, and it was Bill who stepped up and helped me meet our fundraising goals to send a group of children with special needs to summer camp.

Bill and I kept in touch over the next few years, and Bill would occasionally call me to say he was looking for someone "just like me" to come and help him build a new business territory. Each time, I would thank him for reaching out and for the kind words, and then proceed to tell him the 100 reasons why it would never work. I even started sending him prospective job candidates for the opportunity he kept mentioning to me. My mind was closed to options and unwilling to think outside of my current situation.

Time went on, and after selling my most recent business, I decided to take a short breather and focus for a bit on the charity program I had founded and coordinated for a number of years, the MDL Give A Book. I wanted to increase my sponsorships in a new geographic area—the area Bill's office happened to be in. Remembering that he had a kind heart, I called, assuming he'd quickly join me in this mission with only a phone call and a few minutes of explanation.

Instead, Bill asked about my current business, and after hearing I was "in between projects," he asked me to stop by to tell him more about my MDL Give A Book Program in person. Surprised at this extra request, but certainly willing to take a few minutes out of my day to visit Bill in the hopes of securing his sponsorship, I arrived ready to tell him about my program.

After a minute or two, Bill became a sponsor, and after 3 or 4 more hours of our visit, I was finalizing details to join Bill as his new marketing coordinator. I would soon after take the unexpected step way outside my comfort zone to become a loan officer. Coincidence? Perhaps. But my gut tells me there were forces at work that day (along with Bill's "master plan").

My 6:00 AM Facebook Posts

When I decided to join Facebook, I simultaneously made the decision that I was NOT going to be one of the whiners and complainers I had often seen post. I started waking up in the morning and posting some sort of inspirational saying that helped me start that particular day off right. I would get an occasional "like" or comment from a friend, but I honestly never paid much attention to it or gave it a second thought. I posted for me, and if someone else happened to like it too, that was an added bonus.

It wasn't until I took a few days off from posting that I started to realize not only the power of social media, but also the potential power we each have to positively (or negatively) influence our own little piece of the world. I suddenly received several random messages, some from people I hadn't seen or talked to in-person for ages. The specifics were slightly different, but the basic message was the same. They were checking to see if I was ok since I hadn't posted, AND they were telling me about the positive impact my daily messages had on their lives. I was shocked and delighted. To think that something as easy and quick as my Facebook post had positively impacted people got me excited. I was once again reminded of the ripple effect.

> **"Just as ripples spread out when a single pebble is dropped into water, the actions of individuals can have far-reaching effects." - Dalai Lama**

While each of these random stories could certainly be attributed to dumb luck or coincidence, I've noticed that in the past few years as I've gotten much more intentional about the choice I make and the life I am designing, these random coincidences seem to happen more and more frequently.

> **"There are people out there who will NOT become who they are meant to be if you do not become who YOU are supposed to be." - Dani Johnson**

9

LIVING AND LOVING
THE MOMENTS

*"The way we choose to see the world
creates the world we see."*

Barry Neil Kaufman

We can take an important life lesson from the children in our lives. Their minds are so open and ready to learn, experience life, and grow. Everything seems possible for them. They've yet to be jaded by setbacks and disappointments. They are happy, excited, and even giddy to face each new day.

As adults, I believe if we are able to consciously focus on harnessing even a small bit of that excitement and wonderment, our lives could change in a positive way very quickly and dramatically.

A dear friend has a family tradition when a child becomes a teenager. They gather "words of wisdom" from close family and friends and create a special birthday keepsake. I recently came across the message I had written to their daughter, and after a few minor tweaks, I realized it was the same advice and reminders we should all be giving ourselves daily.

Be kind to others, but don't forget to also be kind to yourself. While you're busy taking care of the world and making your little piece of it a better place, remember to also give yourself a break. You will make mistakes along the way. It's part of life's journey, but forgive yourself and move on. Being kind to yourself will allow you the peace and energy to be kind to others too.

Take care of your body. It has to last you a lifetime! Stay active. Eat well. You have so many great adventures ahead, and you'll need your good health to be able to take full advantage of these opportunities as they arise.

Treasure true friendships. Hold on tightly to the friends who make your heart smile, cheer you on, and stick with you through it all. Make them a priority. Take time to stay in touch and support each other through the good, the bad, and everything in-between.

On the other hand, know that there will be lots of people who pass in and out of your life, and that's ok too. You will learn from them all. Some will teach you how to be the person you want to become, and others will show you, by example, what you don't want to become. Both lessons are valuable.

Be true to yourself and follow your heart. I know this one may be the corniest of all, but life will pull you in a million directions, and it will be up to you to decide which way to go, what you stand for, and what matters to you most. Never let fear stop you from taking steps you know are right for you.

Lift other people up. On your journey to be the best you ever, don't forget to bring others along with you. So many think that to reach the top, you have to

81

trample others along the way, but I can tell you that as you lift others up, you will rise too.

Live grateful. No matter how bad a day or a week or a chapter of your life may be, it is all temporary, and there is ALWAYS a reason to be grateful. Take time to find those reasons every day. Grateful thinking will keep you grounded, will help you achieve amazing things, and will even carry you through the hardest times too.

Keep playing. Keep laughing. Keep having fun. Be silly. Be happy. Be you. Yup, it's just that simple.

Do it now! Whatever feels important to you, act on it. Don't wait. When you're young, life feels endless, but it goes by fast. Go out and do it, whatever your "it" may be.

Enjoy the journey. You're busy. You will get busier. While you're busy creating your life ahead, take time to enjoy the moments.

Be present. While technology is amazing, turn it off sometimes and just be in the moment. Enjoy the people and places in your life. Those memories will last you a lifetime.

Celebrate every chance you get. Life will be full of challenges and rough patches. Celebrate all the little triumphs along the way and acknowledge the people in the world who help make those victories possible.

And finally, **choose happy over perfect.** Create a life you design on purpose using your strongest whys to guide you.

I wish you peace, happiness, and all of life's blessings.

With love and smiles,

Wendy

"You are the most important person in your life,
and that doesn't make you selfish.
It makes you stronger, wiser, better."

-Taylor Hentzman,
recalling advice from her
Grandpa Bobby of blessed memory

RESOURCES

Create a daily habit of filling your head with positive messages and new ideas to explore.

Below are links to just a few of the many amazing "gurus" I've enjoyed learning from along my journey. They share their gifts with the world through blogs, podcasts, social media and books. Many of them also interview other amazing guests*.

- ❖ Dani Johnson: www.danijohnson.com

- ❖ Hal Elrod: www.halelrod.com

- ❖ Mitch Matthews: www.mitchmatthews.com

- ❖ Rory Vaden: www.roryvaden.com

- ❖ Tim Ferriss: www.fourhourworkweek.com

- ❖ Niyi Sobo: www.imnotyou.com

- ❖ James Altucher: www.jamesaltucher.com

*The names and links listed on this page are in no way affiliated with Wendy Elover. They are for informational purposes only. Use your own best judgment when signing up for any lists, products,   or   programs.

ABOUT THE AUTHOR

As a speaker, mortgage loan officer and serial entrepreneur, Wendy has had the good fortune to meet and learn from many kind, generous, knowledgeable colleagues and mentors. She hopes to pay it forward by inspiring others to step out of their comfort zones, share their gifts with the world, and create happy lives on purpose.

Wendy attended Rutgers University and earned degrees in business management and business marketing. She later added to her credentials by becoming a certified public accountant (CPA) and mortgage loan officer.

She has owned and operated a number of businesses over the years including an appliance parts store, a CPA practice (with her husband), a marketing company, a fundraising firm and a personalized book and gift business.

Wendy is actively involved in several local business, community, and charitable organizations, and she enjoys creating opportunities for people to pay it forward together.

Wendy founded and coordinates the MDL Give A Book Program (www.ShareTheFunOfReading.com) The program is named in memory of Wendy's mom, Mindy Dorothy Laufer, who volunteered as a literacy volunteer in a local elementary school. The MDL Give A Book gives Wendy the continued opportunity to bring together local business people and special groups of at-risk youngsters to share the excitement and fun of reading together.

Wendy lives in Maryland with her husband and her three daughters, including a set of fraternal twins. In her spare time, Wendy enjoys hanging out with her friends and family, and she feels incredibly grateful and blessed to be living a life she enjoys daily.

LET'S KEEP IN TOUCH

I would love to hear about your journey choosing happy over perfect in your own life. If you'd like to share your thoughts and ideas, or if you'd just like to say hello, contact me at:
wendy@wendyelover.com

To sign up for future bonuses and updates, visit: **www.wendyelover.com**

Interested in having me speak at your event?
Interested in a bulk purchase of books?
Please contact me at: **wendy@wendyelover.com**

Made in the USA
Middletown, DE
17 April 2017